Fire Season

**Previous winners of the
Tupelo Press First / Second Book Award:
The Berkshire Prize**

Jenny Molberg, *Marvels of the Invisible*
Selected by Jeffrey Harrison

Kristina Jipson, *Halve*
Selected by Dan Beachy-Quick

Ye Chun, *Lantern Puzzle*
Selected by D. A. Powell

Mary Molinary, *Mary & the Giant Mechanism*
Selected by Carol Ann Davis and Jeffrey Levine

Daniel Khalastchi, *Manoleria*
Selected by Carol Ann Davis and Jeffrey Levine

Megan Snyder-Camp, *The Forest of Sure Things*
Selected by Carol Ann Davis and Jeffrey Levine

Jennifer Militello, *Flinch of Song*
Selected by Carol Ann Davis and Jeffrey Levine

Kristin Bock, *Cloisters*
Selected by David St. John

Dwaine Rieves, *When the Eye Forms*
Selected by Carolyn Forché

Lillias Bever, *Bellini in Istanbul*
Selected by Michael Collier

David Petruzelli, *Everyone Coming Toward You*
Selected by Campbell McGrath

Bill Van Every, *Devoted Creatures*
Selected by Thomas Lux

Aimee Nezhukumatathil, *Miracle Fruit*
Selected by Gregory Orr

Jennifer Michael Hecht, *The Last Ancient World*
Selected by Janet Holmes

FIRE SEA SON

Patrick Coleman

Tupelo Press
North Adams, Massachusetts

Fire Season.
Copyright © 2018 Patrick Coleman. All rights reserved.

Library of Congress Cataloging-in-Publication Data available upon request.
ISBN: 978-1-946482-15-0

Designed and composed in Calluna Sans and Futura by Josef Beery.
Cover art: Jules Tavernier, *Kilauea Caldera, Sandwich Islands*, 1886,
and Maurice Braun, *Cuyamaca Mountains*, ca. 1920. The San Diego Museum of Art.
Designed by Patrick Coleman.
First edition: December 2018.

Tupelo Press
P.O. Box 1767, North Adams, Massachusetts 01247
(413) 664–9611 / editor@tupelopress.org / www.tupelopress.org

Tupelo Press is an award-winning independent literary press that publishes fine
fiction, nonfiction, and poetry in books that are a joy to hold as well as read.
Tupelo Press is a registered 501(c)(3) nonprofit organization, and we rely on public
support to carry out our mission of publishing extraordinary work that may be
outside the realm of the large commercial publishers. Financial donations are
welcome and are tax deductible.

For Lauren, and to Nora and Alice—
to family is all we can do.

Contents

I wrote these pieces over two years (2012–2014) while working as a low-level curator at the San Diego Museum of Art, an hour away from where I lived in rural Ramona, California. Each was composed aloud into a digital recorder during the drive to and from work, and later transcribed. They are concerned with the local landscapes (literally through which they were written), with the art objects that I encountered on a daily basis, and with the birth of my first child.

—PC

I:

Krishna Swallows the Forest Fire
FROM THE *BHAGAVATA PURANA*
CIRCA 1720
MALWA, INDIA

FIRE SEASON

In the grasslands they put an airport. There's always a good reason. The grasses are dry, golden around the coyotes, late summer. On the drive to work, exhausted, I see two large white planes—heavy-bottomed, boat-like—pass low. On the tails and fuselage are wide orange stripes. They're going to drop water on the wildfires, the wildfires that rained ash over fifty miles onto the hood of my car, the hood of my car that was up to keep rats from chewing the wires, the wires that they've chewed anyways. My wife saw the fire start from where she nursed on the couch. The lightning of a summer thunderstorm that came in from the desert struck the mountain two ranges over. This is in southern California. We have a baby. There's always a fire somewhere, and we spend our days pacing out the distances between there and now.

4

A Divine Gift of One Hundred Honors
GUO HUI
QING DYNASTY
CHINA

DEER IN THE BREAK

Maybe there's music, maybe there's a movie at low volume. Put away the dinner dishes, the meal we ate staggered. My hip is kinked and painful, I don't know why. Think about work. Think about no rest from work, weariness. This is what I want. But still, unfocused desires squeeze through the seams, the vague dissatisfaction that is always mine. Like a hustling retriever, I'm a dog who needs usefulness. Without it, high-strung, hungry, my bearish mind staggers through several campsites, becomes a hummingbird too blighted by possibility to stop and drink, and scatters into light and bone and anything else that fails to form a body. Accept the braces like a field-bound ox. That's goodness. That's the good. Reason is the baby in the bassinet. The fear every time I pass her, it stops me like a deer in the break. Her breathing.

6

A Marble Figure of a Young Satyr Wearing a Theater Mask of Silenus
CIRCA 1ST CENTURY CE
ROMAN EMPIRE

BEING LOST

At yesterday's interdepartmental meeting, several people said, "I don't get why I'm here. What does this meeting have to do with me?" And I, seeing an opportunity for a flatfooted existentialist joke, said, "'Why am I here?' is the question I ask myself every morning when I wake up." Instead of laughter filling the pause I deliberately left, a few kind women said, "Aw." I hadn't meant it, exactly, but we reveal ourselves in tones we didn't intend. Being lost must be mine. But even more miserable and confusing, that these near-strangers, chatterboxes over the coffee machine, sailing along to their own agendas—printed and imagined, dictated and dreamed—are there to receive and to respond not with distance or a joke, as I would, but kindly. Still, the sentimental me writing this now shouldn't forget that we spent the next hour and a half planning to procure eighty thousand dollars from area philanthropists, large and small, in order to purchase new desks, because the current ones were not sexy enough.

Sacrifice of Isaac
JEAN CHARLOT
1933

THE FIFTH OF MAY

It was my father's birthday, it was the fifth of May. The moon was the closest it'd be to the earth for another something years. The heat had gone, replaced by a cold that reminded me of summers at a lake, the cold of a thing resting at the bottom of a lake. And here we were: my family. And you. You, with whom I'd left the operating room containing the woman I love most. I remember your face hard enough I see it everywhere—a memory fundamental, firmamental enough to map your features onto the road I drive, the distant hills I used to want to hike, the body of every woman and girl on every sidewalk and shopping aisle. A week passes from your birth, and the moon is the closest it'll ever be to us, your face is there too in its craters, and then it will be moving away—and I'll be going back to work, and you'll draw closer to your mother, the best person I know, how it should be, and that's good, that's what I want. But it's also the first loss I'll spend the rest of our lives trying to make up for.

I Was Always Present
GEORGE GROSZ
1942

THE USUAL

In the familiar mottled light of another new day I wonder if I
can be stranger, could be unusualed.

Kilauea Caldera, Sandwich Islands
JULES TAVERNIER
1886

AUDIO TOUR FOR WHEREVER YOU ARE

Look down. Get real quiet. Feel the throbbing of hell beneath your feet. Know that only 144,000 were chosen to enter heaven. Know that God chose them before time began grinding into beings, that nothing you can do will change that. Know that 107 billion people lived and died before today, that the quota may have already been reached. So either prepare yourself for a long damnation or put it out of your head, try to ease the meantime for some other people headed toward the same end. Or, if you're an atheist, please visit the gift shop. All exhibition catalogues are 50% off.

Atheism
JIM DINE
1986

GROUND AND FIGURE

I take off my robe to make coffee. There's another solution, but I fill the grinder and fold the robe over it, again, again, and can't find the button to make it start through layers of fleece. If I've done a good job, the grinder is muffled, and you will keep sleeping. The unfolding is done just as carefully. Removing the filled lid is like sliding bars of uranium out of a nuclear reactor. So is taking a cup from the cabinet. If I'm who I regularly expect myself to be, I fail. If I'm as good as I sometimes hope I am, all of this happens without a sound. Days you wake, we let your mother sleep. I slide your bassinet into the kitchen, singing. Bassinet, the baby basin. Cabinet, the baby cabin. Everything is offspringing. I tell you, This is how we make toast. This is what butter smells like when it's melting. I tell you, This is how we make coffee. This time, I leave my robe on when I grind the roasted beans to dust. These are things I want you to hear.

16

The Virgin and Child
BASAWAN
FROM THE JAHANGIR ALBUM, 1590
INDIA

BREAKING GROUND

I dug a garden bed for you. It was eight feet long and ten feet wide. Your grandfather's going to plant potatoes there. It won't have a fence, like the other garden; if the squirrels and kangaroo rats and gophers want to take their share, we're going to share. While I turned earth that had never been turned, your mother sat in the blue padded rocker and fed you from her body. Her act is one embodied in emblems and art since the beginning of time: a woman, a breast, a baby. Maybe one day you'll feed your child this way, too, and remembering that pose is my way of wishing you strength. Me, I did other things. I fed your mother brownies, changed your diapers. I cooked a lot of food. And I made a garden bed. Each of the three days I dug it, I planned on telling your mother, when she asked how it went that day, that it wasn't groundbreaking. It's a dumb joke you'll come to recognize as in my dumb-joke style. Coming back in, I forgot to say it each day.

Pool in the Mountains
MILTON AVERY
1950

FIRE SEASON

Breath on the water. Molecules touching molecules making friction, making surfaces shift, making things happen. The helicopter drinks from the cattle pond settled among a long trajectory of blonde grasslands, kindling. Blades displace air which displaces water, animating its surfaces and the light it reflects. A plume of smoke from out past the airport. We're going to the park and thinking about frustration, and now we're heading up the hill for a better vantage, thinking: wind direction, temperature and humidity, potential timelines, roads it will leap, what unsurvivable losses will we pack into the trunk. The cat, of course. Now pictures of you—an endless number, it seems like, but no, it's finite, and they're stored on hard drives. The beginning of your life and the tone of those first days is ready to be reconjured by a magnet skimming a hairsbreadth over a cycling plastic circle, a push and pull of sympathetic and unsympathetic invisible fields outputting a line-by-line facsimile of your face, mine, your mother's, hospital scrubs, and the nauseous awe that confirms the unknowable drop of each life into itself and then out again. The traffic is stopped at the highway. People are out of their cars, watching the diving planes and helicopters. Whose home. What lives. And such strangeness in this one, to stand later in a checkout line and look across the store over crates of dry goods to see my wife, arms folded before a rotating display of potato chips that twirls and twirls, and to know, without seeing, your happiness at having discovered this wheeling and what it has to do with your hand.

Portrait of Monsieur Monteux
PIERRE BONNARD
1915

TRKLDWN

When the old man driving the Jaguar passes you with a license plate that says TRKLDWN, he must mean piss, the loosening of the musculature from an inflamed prostate, the little bit of pee that comes out after he's tucked back into his pants.

Landscape
MING DYNASTY, 17TH CENTURY
CHINA

EQUIVALENTS

Coming down the mountain, rain pouring on the distant valley looks like badly done Photoshop—overblurred edges of the superimposed clouds. Badly done Photoshop looks like rain pouring on the distant valley as you come down from the mountain.

Lyrisches
VASILY KANDINSKY
FROM THE SUITE *KLÄNGE*
1913

BUCOLIC

Every morning I drive past wild horses on the way to work. I never stop. It's never too hot nor too cold, but still I don't get out, even when there are colts, fresh-limbed and bolting all the wild grass the last protected wild grassland in California can offer. These are lucky horses, in a way. Moved here, protected by fences, photographed often, Facebooked. I should see myself so lucky as well. I have 187 friends, plus or minus two, depending on whether I've posted something political recently. Am I proud? No. Do I make any change? Not for more than an hour. Do I want to? Yes. Do the colts want to change? The colts don't need to change. They're there in the field, nuzzling their mothers' kneecaps, testing out new limbs, and wondering in some inarticulate horse language what wonderful things they can do with these legs.

The Primal Wing
AGNES PELTON
1933

INACCURATE ART HISTORY

Before the sunrise, in the sky Agnes Pelton made, we saw a crow cross the face of the moon. I don't ask what these signs mean anymore. Like her, I grew up under these kinds of skies, like you will, too. Their habitual coming and going make them like nothing, but they're something to me now. Agnes Pelton was from Cathedral City. She must have gone away, too. How else would she have been moved by these desert colors enough to spend her life remaking them? Do you smell the sage, or has it already faded to backdrop for more novel sensations? Symbols and ideas only take you so far. Pelton painted the sky because she had found it again—because it had not been hers to see for a time, and then it was, once more. She painted so as not to lose it all over again. Except that isn't right, Pelton worked in Cathedral City but wasn't from there, I misremembered, so what does that mean? I accept at times that ideas are stronger than truth, as much as I accept that one day you'll need to leave this place to return. Death may be the same. Under these desert lights we fill ourselves with longing for a place without existence, so familiar and so faint.

Mission Valley in Flood
MAURICE BRAUN
UNDATED

SOD, STARS

In the books, you know the names of all the pictures but cannot speak them, know even the three places the bug is hiding (only part of a face in profile, protruding from behind the sink), which is a fact hard to fathom, a difficult depth to plumb, visible in these azure-colored, tiger's eye flashes of brilliance playing the surfaces of your being—a formulation like Northern Lights in which radiation interacts with particulates to produce mutable wonder and, to think of it, this isn't the worst metaphor for your eyes (though eye metaphors are especially perilous) because, to speak non-metaphorically, they have no stable color but are what most often people call gray, silver, gray-hazel, dull blue, partly green and partly golden brown. It's impossible to speak non-figuratively. So when I say we went outside just past sunset and looked down into the soft agricultural valley, with its shimmering surfaces of watered sod, and when we looked at the sky, which was some kind of blue, some kind of gray, some kind of gold, and I said the stars weren't out yet, and it was close to bedtime, so would you like to come see them with me another night when you were up later or the sun went to bed earlier, you knew what we were talking about. You pointed up and said, "Tars, tars, tars."

Shono: Driving Rain
UTAGAWA HIROSHIGE
CIRCA 1833

DEVELOPMENTAL GRAMMAR

"I don't have stars on my hands, I have rain on my umbrella."

(She was looking at her own waterspeckled palms.)

II:

Still-life Synchromy with Nude in Yellow
MORGAN RUSSELL
1913

ALICE, WONDER

Like honeymoon sex, the belief that a cock can enter over and over again till eternity, no change, the clock counts counterclockwise, with hands that run counter to convention, too. We bought it on our honeymoon. Newly committed, convinced there would always be more time, we spent the week eating Thai food and watching *The Tyra Banks Show* and walking along a seashore that ebbed and flowed into the same positions two times a day. Our daughter now talks. She points to the clock and says, "Cock." The clock is broken, hands tangled at midnight. The Cheshire cat that decorates its face grins, and grins, and grins, and grins, and grins, and grins, and grins, and then vanishes.

Thanksgiving Still Life
EMIL CARLSEN
1891

THAT SAYING

Call it anti-social. Call it an introvert's need. Call it a mostly managed lineage and personal history of alcohol abuse. But *sláinte*, I think, on the eve of an in-lawed Thanksgiving while mashing eight pounds of boiled red potatoes. I've poured myself a whiskey, away from the family who enjoy each other's company on the other side of the house. I am in quiet and in contact with myself, with that net of relation hanging nearby, calling me back. Then, on a romantic impulse and because I've never done it, I open the back door and stand on the bank above the California lilac that this time of year sets no trace of fragrance on the wind. I say it again—it's absurd for me to say anyway, the cultural affectation of a third-generation fractional Irish—and pour out a splash of whiskey. It penetrates crumbling soil, and the scent rises up from the dirt, and so does my grandmother, eight years gone. She taught me that saying on the eve of my first trip to Dublin, taught me to drink well and what that tasted like. These spirits do something, persist; they find what parts of her remain in the earth. There she is, and the grandfather who made her and made her read the bookie's tote board when he went blind, and those who made him and their mothers, and some inkling of their lives, and some momentary touch of an ancestral whole, the *slán*. I'm feeding them, they're hungry, and so am I. And so is my family next door, to whom I will return with potatoes and whiskey on my breath, and later—much later—with less—much less—but with some trace of the same.

Light Area, Motion in Space
OSKAR FISCHINGER
1944

DEVELOPMENTAL GRAMMAR

"All the reindeer love him, all the reindeer love him, all the reindeer love him, and coffee, and coffee, and hand."

Isadora Duncan
JOHN SLOAN
1915

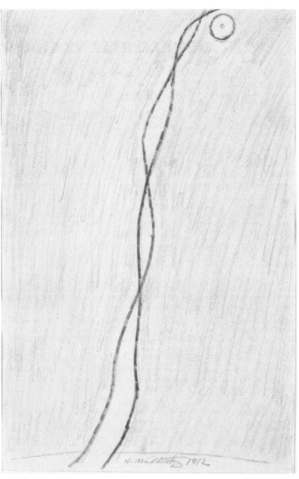

Isadora Duncan
ABRAHAM WALKOWITZ
1912

ON ICE

This girl can make a tile floor an ice-skating rink, and I see a rock
and say, Rock, rock, rock, rock, rock. One of us has magic and
the other a stutter, a neurotic hitch of finding realness as most
basic. In simple things. But the little girl sliding is all vector and
joy and earthbound toe-loops. She doesn't have direction but is
one. Like the river. Like the river. Like the river in all seasons but
deep winter, when it becomes ice and a memorial to motion.
Like a headstone. Like a rock.

The Shadows
RENÉ MAGRITTE
1966

EQUIVALENTS

With sun rising behind thin clouds to illuminate the trees on the mountaintop at the desertward terminus of the grasslands valley, each articulated contour of the conifers is the tiny tooth of a dollhouse saw used to cut the miniature Christmas tree in half before dragging it to the curb for the rare, twice-yearly over-sized pick-up. Christmas trees waiting for the rare, twice-yearly over-sized pick-up are the contours of the dollhouse saw of the ridgeline conifers at the desertward terminus of the grasslands valley, with sun rising behind, illuminating, articulated.

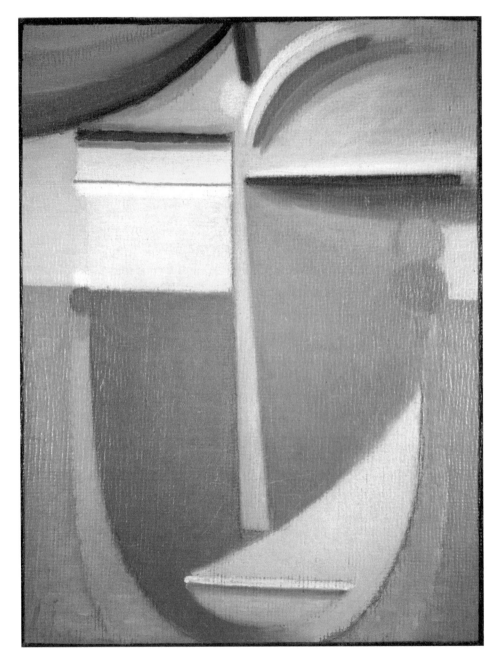

Abstract Head: Inner Vision
ALEXEI JAWLENSKY
1923

DEVELOPMENTAL GRAMMAR

"I'm a guitar. This is my instrument."

(She pointed to my mouth.)

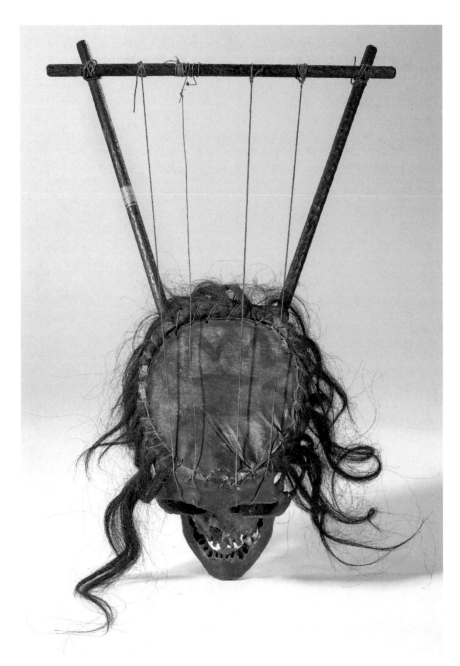

Lyre
19TH CENTURY
CENTRAL AFRICA

AND NOW I AM THEIR SONG

Whose song am I? From whose lips do I fly in sorrow, pity, rage, or fear—or why not love? Why is love the last to come to mind? It should be simplest. From my wife a ballad, direct, and deliberately paced—sung in clear voice, no vibrato, but with the earnest timbre and dignity of labor long sought, our labor—to find each other, to make some harmony between us— the labor that brought one child into the world and that will, God willing, bring another. My daughter would sing me as the Bare Necessities, punctuated by the tone of childlike surprise at discovering another's words inside oneself. (Can it be childlike when it comes from a child? But childish isn't right either.) My parents might sing my praises, but if they sing me, it's likely only a song of sadness, of loss, of why-doesn't-he-come-around- more—which is, strictly speaking, more a song of them. But I'm not a song in the sense Job was the tune of his tormentors, of the torment and the source of torment itself. I have no enemies. I have few relationships in which I've behaved despicably badly, which doesn't make me good. Only quiet. Conflict-avoidant. Something nearer silence. If asked to sing me my friends would sing that I am the song of the slow slip-away, of the forgot- to-return-a-call, of the I-wonder-what-happened-to-him. It's a standard. A standby. A series of notes to fail against. To improvise upon. To improve.

Monkey Antiquarian
FOLLOWER OF JEAN-BAPTISTE-SIMÉON CHARDIN
AFTER 1740

ARSE POETICA

When your boss throws you under the bus—the latest bump, you, in a highway of grievances, fuck-offs and resignations you rehearse both ways along the actual, pot-holed road—it's best to wonder what kind. If it's mine, let it be a Greyhound filled with people who only have one thing in common. Destination: Big Sur. If hers, let it be the short kind. And yes, I guess I'm taking the opportunity to defend the right of the poet to make an ugly, cruel joke, or at least to let it slip and have the decency not to pretend it didn't. But don't mistake mistake for a well-thought-through position. Things are said in anger that wouldn't be said in, well. You know. And if you don't, go fuck yourself.

The Beginning of Life
FRANTIŠEK KUPKA
1900–03

AUDIO TOUR FOR WHEREVER
YOU ARE

Look up. Looking up makes you feel better. It's psychological. But if you were to travel along your eyes' path, imagine your end: in a star, ashed like a cigarette; drawn into a black hole; or plowed into the surface of another material body. You're on your way to it. We sent you out, but we're going to bring you back alive. Do you hear me, Lieutenant? I need you to breathe. I need you to slow down. Orient yourself back on that little blue dot. Tell me what it looks like from up there. Tell me what you see. Lieutenant? Tell me what you see.

I was not wanted. I was a gift upon the earth.

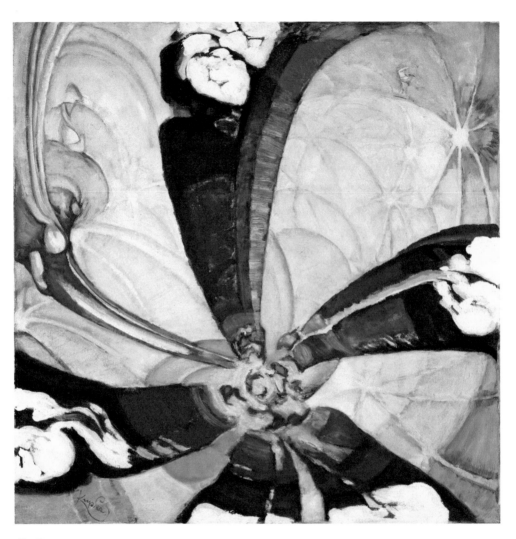

Blue Space
FRANTIŠEK KUPKA
CIRCA 1912

THE LAST OCEAN

Out of the pages of a book you pull a penguin from the diminishing ice pack of the most untouched (but still touched) wilderness. You hold it in your small palm, pet its invisible back, ask me to kiss its invisible beak, and say, "It's so cute, it's so cute, it's so cute." Humans have long over-handled the world, with the same effect as when making a grandmother's pie crust— tried to hold too much and let go less. Before it gets worse, you hold invisibly: to witness, to proclaim, to share.

Mon destin me crie de le suivre . . . . lâchez moi, Messieurs, ou par le Ciel, je ferai un fantôme du premier qui m'arrêtera.

Hamlet Tries to Follow His Father's Ghost
EUGÈNE DELACROIX
1835

DEVELOPMENTAL GRAMMAR

"I have a secret. It's called me and Daddy."

Nude
CHRISTIAN ROHLFS
1911

ABIDE WITH ME

When one abides, one elides to make the daily doing survivable. Plied with failures, IOUs, past-due notices, and dishes piled higher than what was once in your childhood known as Sears Tower, which was once the tallest building, one who abides needs more than patience, needs pride. Each other is his or her bestmost self in any given moment. That may be sad depending on whom you're sitting near. But sit with it until it ceases being torment. There's good in everything, lying dormant. Or awake, cautiously taking steps, then retreating like a dormouse. Abiding gives it space, a house interrupting chainless, arid desert, four walls a pausing place, a place for wondering—the painting above the potbellied stove making one ask, Who was she on her best days?

Farm Landscape, Cattle in Pasture, Sunset Nantucket
GEORGE INNESS
CIRCA 1883

DEVELOPMENTAL GRAMMAR /
EQUIVALENTS

While brushing your teeth, you waved the brush in the air before you, saying, "I'm painting, I'm painting." Making circles: "It's a house." A smaller circle: "It's a door." Then with your fist: "Knock knock knock."

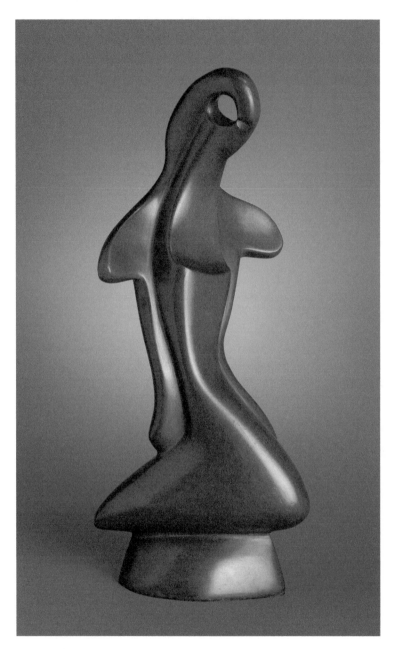

Leda and the Swan
ALEXANDER ARCHIPENKO
CIRCA 1938

LEDA AND . . .

A swan. Made of glass the size and sheen of a thumbnail, it lived for years in the soil of a pot, at the base of a trailing vine, and had traveled that way both ways across the country with a clay raccoon and a pewter cat. It was the cat, the living one, that knocked the pot to the ground. The first time all was fine. I found the swan next to the bookcase, near the eighty-year-old editions of *The Wizard of Oz* and *Ramona* and *Jane Eyre*, these books that belong to so many girlhoods, even those of boys. The second time the wings broke from the tiny glass swan. It was our anniversary. I told you and you cried and fed the baby. Your grandmother, long dead, gave the swan to you in your girlhood, the same grandmother who shared those books of hers. Our daughter grew fussy and, the way she does these days, began pointing at everything she wanted, which was everything: string, lamp, sumac leaves, puzzle. What she wanted wouldn't stay still so I couldn't satisfy her, and she cried. Love is dropping into an abyss edged with a hundred jutting branches and choosing instead to hold the circle of daylight above, the image that grows smaller and smaller as you fall: moon, dime, bead, star, pinprick, memory. How could I have known the glass swan was one such fixed point in your sky? Asking, paying attention, remembering. You had told me before.

Female Nude
EDWARD BURNE-JONES
UNDATED

BIBLIOGRAPHIC RESEARCH

There are the masterpieces, but mostly there are drawings, etchings, lithographs, linocuts, and watercolors—works on paper that can only withstand the light for so long and evince an artist working things out quickly and then into the next moment, if not before canceling a misshapen face or feature first with a slashed X. Among these one finds overwhelmingly the female body. It's a marvel, all these men (its mostly men but women, too) and the hours they've spent sketching breasts, nipples, hips in various state of contortion, feet rubbing together or knees parted, eyes averted, eyes on me, and hair—I don't much notice the hair. That says something about me, and it says something about you, my wife, my love, to whom each of these hand-worked figures immutably corresponds. Why don't I write more about you? I'm not an artist. I wouldn't know what to do with a live nude model in the corner of my studio. I need distance, loss, or its possibility; I need the world to cede to mind and memory. You're here, and I never don't know it. In this there's a poetics, I'm sure, but one that only reaches these typing hands in touching you: of you and how I want you.

Stormy Sky of Frisian Farmhouse
EMIL NOLDE
CIRCA 1935

DEVELOPMENTAL GRAMMAR

"That tree burned in the fire. Where is the fire now?"

III:

Waiting for Her in "Love's Sacred Thicket"
NAINSUKH
LATE 18TH CENTURY
GULER, INDIA

DEACCESSIONING

It is spring, the red-winged blackbirds glitch the silence, and everything is a work of art: The cowpond at sunset anchors a landscape of George Inness, and at midday, in the wash of a less diluted light, it's the mountain pond Milton Avery staked out. The bands of green, darker along the ridgeline, are hills an atelier of artists in Guler would have found delightful for the ways in which they allow for the creation of dimension—before the Rajput palace was abandoned and the workshop artists scattered to draw picture postcards for tourists in pencil on beige Dutch paper. Yesterday I washed my car. My daughter, wearing only a shirt, crouched slightly and pissed on the ground. She took pleasure in watching her own springing pool and how quickly the heat reduced it to a darker patch of pink-stained concrete—her shadow, she said, waving to it. Kupka found his way into pure color, motion, movement, the passage of time, and something like transcendence through pencil sketches of a nude girl playing with a ball. My child forgets her shadow while it evaporates, lost in the sparkle of the young, individually articulated leaves in the windblown trees. A blue-skinned god would have delighted to make love under these, as the river Yamuna runs by—yielding nothing to opaque watercolor and gold and beetle-wing casings, to the hands of an artist moved by all this ever beginning.

70

The Hands of Dr. Moore
DIEGO RIVERA
1940

SNOT EPISTEMOLOGY (PART I)

There's so much love for the body. Two years ago my brother
wrapped his son in a towel after the bath, and the boy tripped
on the shower coping and landed teeth-first. Between then and
now they watched the gums bruise and fade to pink before a
blackness blossomed under the enamel. My brother, the dentist,
pulled them from his child's mouth by force. The boy had leapt
into the chair, held the mirror, watched the procedure as pure
pleased attention. The two teeth, trailing long tendrils of
diseased root like dollhouse bindles of ginger, he placed under
his pillow in hopes of a tooth fairy's five bucks.

Woman, Bird, Constellations
JOAN MIRÓ
1974

SNOT EPISTEMOLOGY (PART II)

Ideas, too, should get their due. Tonight, sitting in a nest of pillows, you said, "I'm Big Bird! I'm Big Bird! Rock a-bye baby! Rock a-bye baby! I rock! I rock! I rock! I quack! Quack! Quack! Bawk! Bawk! Bawk! I'm Big Bird! I'm Nora!" You hopped from the bed and draped your blanket over your head, tripped on its tail and cracked your beak against the tile. When you rose up, blood trailed across your cheeks, blood you smeared in tears over your eyes so your skin was jeweled like a prizefighter's sweat. This is the human water of pain, ornamented in red by the transports of your being, your breath, which became ATP and muscle contraction and a wail you left in the air at that moment forever, a wail that echoes in its instant of What-happened and Will-it-stop-hurting. Your mom got a towel, and I wiped your face. I folded the blood from your nose into the rag, but through your sobs you asked to see inside. When I opened the rag, there in red and pink against the white, glistening like a fresh oyster, was the shape of your blood and mucus—all those things skin can truly be said to hold. Despite my expectation, this calmed you. You touched it delicately with the print of your finger. "It's a heart, Daddy," you said and cried a little longer, but more softly now, softer, and under the conversation of color and shape.

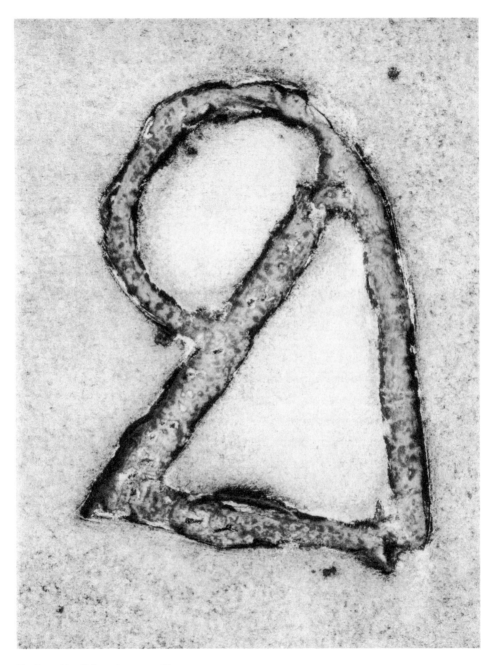

The fire guides all throughout everything . . .
FRANÇOIS FIEDLER
1973

AUDIO TOUR FOR WHEREVER YOU ARE

Find the smallest thing you can see: dust mote, sand grain, hair follicle. Imagine being small enough that to traverse it would take an entire day. The dust has its own dust, the sand its own softness in admixture, the hair its own tectonics as you find yourself risen by evening, shaved down in the predawn. Each molecule of atmosphere buffets you more particularly now, though not particularly enough. Smallness has its virtue, its helpless sifting to the sediment of complexity. It seems easier to find enough at that size, a sack a flour a lifetime supply. You could pass unseen through the world, and live however you saw fit—and fitting is different when you could walk between the pages of a closed book. Walk through them now. Find each letter a monolith, an abstract monument to animal sound, the A for, Are you there? I am. I am.

Awakening
GUTZON BORGLUM
1911

EQUIVALENTS

The banked facade of the marine layer abutting the foothills is like the dust cloud rolling across the Central Valley bringing valley fever. Valley fever is a banked facade of marine layer settling over the cooling body where it meets the heat of outer light.

After Many Days
THOMAS HART BENTON
1940

EAT EAT

for J. L.

They lost him. After fifteen years, an accident. That's all. If this is a world in which a child can be lost, then this isn't a world. It's a scrim, a mutable cloth, an unfurled bolt of many folds, creases, and thread counts. And death is a bundling of the textile, and loss is a design's temporary resignation to darkness. Pull it tight. Lay it upon the table, then bring out the light. Trace the patterns and the colors, these colors we're left searching for, and decide for what sick feast this setting is fit.

Krishna and the cowherds enter Agasura's mouth
FROM THE BHAGAVATA PURANA
CIRCA 1800
DATIA, INDIA

FIRE SEASON

How the teeth and how the nails and how the cock that claims.
How the hate of impure things; how to hate one's remains. How
to eat and how the hunger draws ease from pain. I saw a mouth
with thirty-three teeth and its throat was the center of me, and
the teeth—how the teeth, how the teeth—frame all I see.

Apollo and Daphne
PAULO CALIARI, KNOWN AS VERONESE
CIRCA 1560–65

CURING OLIVES

Every week he hand-sprayed the trees with kaolin clay, which dried fruit-boring pests to death. We helped pick the bright green, almost apple-like olives a little too early; he was heading east to a son's big Philadelphia wedding, they'd be bad by his return. Each of us had two buckets: one for good fruit, one for the infested. Later, after getting you to sleep, I went to the man's garage. He and his wife were stark under the droplights. Halved plastic jugs hung from the ceiling. IV lines dripped green, viscous fluid into pails. They ground olives to pulp, separated the oil in food processors, and filtered it down through the milk jugs and surgical tubing. Because of the early harvest, the oil was ghastly bitter. Maybe it would mellow. If they worked all night, they would get through a tenth of what they'd grown—the rest, left to rot. The press in town had tried to claim half their crop, but they preferred doing things like this: with not enough time. I was there to take home a few gallons of raw olives, to help mitigate the disaster through the acceptance of generosity. This is how harvest turns to slough, and slough to harvest— each marked by a little losing, a little loss. Those olives are now packed in jars of brine, green and rose-hued, surrounded with lemon wedges, garlic, mustard seed, bay leaves, and chilies. I keep them in a back cabinet, out of the light. But every week or two I pull a jar out. The fruit seems to glow, to be aware of its miraculous survival and the waste that caught the others, the wreckage they've made it beyond, for now, and the kind of despoilage that may still be to come.

Prometheus Making Man and Animating Him with Fire from Heaven
AFTER HENDRICK GOLTZIUS
1589

FIRE SEASON

Two fires burn, transmuting sagebrush and oakwood into smoke and ash and other floating bodies that rose to appear, from this vantage, like two towers on the same morning a blue line tells us what my wife's body had already suggested, that another new life is knitting itself together. New life. New life isn't right. Like fate or simple deterministic causality, nothing new is under the skin, only one life careening into another, each simultaneously devouring its twin and giving something different a chance to begin. As two fires become six, the winds scrape my sinuses raw and irritability replaces the joy of news. The numerical odds of randomness dwindle and the ash columns point toward arson, a psychopath with a carton of cigarettes flicking butts out the window along the highways. Multiply. Multiply. Multiply. It's so easy for a man to spread his seed, and the children that will rise up there, and the terrain they'll leave to smolder. Home fires turn to wild fires become home fires again. The smoke towers, with or without a flame, and the stems and branches stem and branch, even in drought, even in death, whatever the fuck that means. Sometime later, wildflowers will blaze on the hillsides unbelievably before the taller plants rekindle and leaf and make some goddamn shade, relief.

86

Night Rain at Ōyama
UTAGAWA TOYOKUNI II
FROM THE SERIES *EIGHT FAMOUS VIEWS OF KANAGAWA*
CIRCA 1830

EQUIVALENTS

Rain slicks on rooftops lit by full light look like solar panels for everyone. Everyone's solar panels look like rain slicks on rooftops catching the light.

The Fall of the Rebel Angels,
PARADISE LOST, BOOK 1, LINE 44
JOHN MARTIN
UNDATED

FALSE EQUIVALENTS

Why air and not airs? Why you and not yous? A fire is always fires but we're relieved when there's only one. False singulars. A dropped "s" to obscure the onslaughting passage of the many among the many.

Aeneas and His Family Fleeing Troy
SIMON VOUET
CIRCA 1635–40

PUSH

A nurse had taken us into a second room. The door shut behind us. The nurse said, "I need you to open that door for me." All the walls were white. Not only were all the walls white, all the walls were walls. There was no door anywhere, not even the one we came in through. There were thin black vertical seams every few feet, but there were no handles, no knobs, no bar that said "push here." I asked the nurse where the door was and she said, "There," without taking her hands from the bassinet. "Where?" "There," she said again. She said it three times. I looked down at you, staring at me peacefully, waiting for me to see the door and to usher you through it. One minute away from your mother with you and I was already lost. Now annoyed, the nurse said, "Just step forward and push." "On that wall?" I asked. "Yes," she said. I took a step away from you and, overwhelmed, confused, so completely living in my eyes, pushed on the wall that I was sure was a wall, and it swung out onto the familiar hallway and the rest of the world to come.

Cuyamaca Mountains
MAURICE BRAUN
CIRCA 1920

COMMUTED

Fall has begun. Instead of the long hour of highway home, I go to the grasslands and lace up my fifteen-dollar running shoes. A commute, commuted. Cattle graze here. A plastic split-rail fence, undegradable, separates the trail from their greenest pasture where the creek runs from the duck pond. Two calves are on the wrong side of it, so I hop the fence, take the long way around. My lungs keep finding air where a month ago I found only bile and shame and a sense of my own pathetic aging. Having made the loop, I come upon the cattle once again. A mother nuzzles her infant's belly. I think of my wife and daughter, at home now, waiting for me only five minutes away, and how all distances are now measured as time. Then the cow nuzzles further and nips at her daughter's teat, it's not wrong, I think of the Muslim man arrested for kissing his infant son, among other places, on the penis. Love finds eternal summer where others find a warm day, a warm day, a warm day, too many tourists, then a cooling trend. I love my Bess, who is bovine only in how her painful tenderness conceals the tough muscle of her oversized heart, and our little Clara the calfling. The starlings murmurate eastward toward Mount Woodson and the setting sun that will not settle. Our patch of earth turns away only to face it again a dozen hours farther along, while this star, this star, this star looks out, looks out, looks out, and won't quit, not for a billion years. Now that I have, I won't.

A lion made from calligraphy
CIRCA 1800
INDIA

FIRE SEASON

The stripes are red, not orange. We discover this one Sunday morning at the airport. The cows graze just beyond the runway, no fence between. I tell you about the planes, about the tubes running to them like mamas feeding their babies, filling their bellies with water that they'll carry over the tinderbox landscape and use to extinguish these occasional, temporary eruptions into fire. But the stripes on the plane that I saw from great distance another morning two years ago, when you were new born, appeared orange to my eye and mind. Maybe every thought's a mistake. Maybe fire is perpetual—everpresent—and suckling grass, snowblooming coyote bush, dapplethrowing oak leaves in the treetops, any kind of verdure and days like these with you, who points at these steel albatrosses and says, "Water in their bellies, water in their bellies," is an instant of peace in a horizon of burning. Maybe today is the event of the season, the temporary tent erected over the collapsible amphitheater. There are limits to what language can do, limits to how perception bends, and then no. Let me applaud while the show unfolds. Let you enjoy as many encores as these performers' bodies can will out. Let the crew, waiting in the wings to tear this whole production down, lean into their cigarettes, and let improbably long columns of ash cling to the filters. If they rush this stage, let me have the strength to hold them back as long as my heart will last. The lion leaps through this ring of fire for your wonder; the lion is stationary, and the fire leaps. Let's watch them do it again.

Art Sources and Permissions

"Fire Season" ("In the grasslands . . .")
Krishna swallows the forest fire, from the Bhagavata Purana ("Ancient Text of the Lord"). India, Malwa, circa 1720. Opaque watercolor and gold on paper. The San Diego Museum of Art; Edwin Binney 3rd Collection, 1990.968.

"Deer in the Break"
Guo Hui. *A Divine Gift of One Hundred Honors*. China, Qing dynasty. Ink and colors on silk hanging scroll, 76 3/4 x 44 1/8 in. (194.95 x 112.08 cm). The San Diego Museum of Art; Museum purchase with funds provided by Rosalyn and Daniel Jacobs, 2002.2.

"Being Lost"
A Marble Figure of a Young Satyr Wearing a Theater Mask of Silenus, Roman Imperial, circa 1st century A.D., with restorations by Alessandro Algardi, 1628. Courtesy of Sotheby's, Inc. Copyright © 2013.

"The Fifth of May"
Jean Charlot. *Sacrifice of Isaac*, 1933. Lithograph proof, 8 x 6 1/8 in. (20.32 x 15.56 cm). The San Diego Museum of Art; Gift of Mr. Jack Lord, 1972.244.h. Copyright © 2018 The Jean Charlot Estate LLC / Member, Artists Rights Society (ARS), NY. Used with permission.

"The Usual"
George Grosz. *I Was Always Present*, 1942. Oil on canvas, mounted on panel, 35 3/4 x 27 7/8 in. Hecksher Museum of Art. Copyright © Estate of George Grosz/Licensed by VAGA, New York, NY.

"Audio Tour for Wherever You Are" ("Look down . . .")
Jules Tavernier. *Kilauea Caldera, Sandwich Islands*, 1886. Oil on canvas, 27 5/8 x 56 3/8 in. (70.17 x 143.19 cm). The San Diego Museum of Art; Museum purchase with funds provided by Kevin and Tamara Kinsella, 2002.35.

"Ground and Figure"
Jim Dine. *Atheism*, 1986. Lithograph proof, 67 x 47 1/16 in. (170.18 x 119.54 cm). The San Diego Museum of Art; Museum purchase, 1992.2. Copyright © 2018 Jim Dine / Artists Rights Society (ARS), New York.

"Breaking Ground"
Basawan. *The Virgin and Child*, from the Jahangir Album. India, 1590. Opaque watercolor and gold on paper, 8 17/32 x 5 13/32 in. (21.7 x 13.7 cm). The San Diego Museum of Art; Edwin Binney 3rd Collection, 1990.293.

"Fire Season: ("Breath on the water . . .")
Milton Avery. *Pool in the Mountains*, 1950. Oil on canvas, 30 3/16 in. x 40 1/8 in. (76.68 cm x 101.92 cm). The San Diego Museum of Art; Gift of Mr. and Mrs. Norton S. Walbridge, 1991.9. Copyright © 2018 The Milton Avery Trust / Artists Rights Society (ARS), New York.

"TRKLDWN"
Pierre Bonnard. *Portrait of Monsieur Monteux*, 1915. Oil on canvas, 32 1/4 x 26 7/8 in. (81.92 x 68.26 cm). The San Diego Museum of Art; Gift of Ambassador and Mrs. Maxwell Gluck, 1981.85. Copyright © 2018 Artists Rights Society (ARS), New York.

"Equivalents" ("Coming down the mountain . . .")
Landscape, Ming dynasty, 17th century, China. Ink on paper, hanging scroll, 65 7/8 x 14 3/4 in. (167.32 x 37.47 cm). The San Diego Museum of Art; Gift of Mr. S. M. Hsiao, Hong Kong.

"Bucolic"
Vasily Kandinsky. *Lyrical* (Lyrisches) (plate, folio 9), from Klänge (Sounds), 1913. Woodcut. Museum of Modern Art. Copyright © 2018 Artists Rights Society (ARS), New York.

"Inaccurate Art History"
Agnes Pelton. *The Primal Wing*, 1933. Oil on canvas, 24 x 25 in. (60.96 x 63.5 cm). The San Diego Museum of Art; Gift of the artist, 1934.12.

"Sod, Stars"
Maurice Braun. *Mission Valley in Flood*, n.d. Oil on canvas, 18 1/4 x 22 1/8 in. (46.36 x 56.2 cm). The San Diego Museum of Art; Museum purchase through the Otto H. Schneider Fund, 1974.19.

"Developmental Grammar" ("I don't have stars on my hands . . .")
Utagawa Hiroshige. *Shono: Driving Rain*, circa 1833. Woodblock, 8 7/8 x 13 3/4 in. (22.54 x 34.93 cm). The San Diego Museum of Art; Bequest of Mrs. Cora Timken Burnett, 1957.236.

"Alice, Wonder"
Morgan Russell. *Still-life Synchromy with Nude in Yellow*, 1913. Oil on canvas, 39 1/4 x 31 1/2 in. (99.7 x 80.01 cm). The San Diego Museum of Art; Museum purchase through the Earle W. Grant Endowment Fund, 1973.22.

"That Saying"
Emil Carlsen. *Thanksgiving Still Life*, 1891. Oil on canvas, 46 x 42 in. (116.84 x 106.68 cm). The San Diego Museum of Art; Gift of Mr. Melville Klauber in memory of his wife, Amy Salz Klauber, 1928.80.

"Developmental Grammar" ("All the reindeer love him . . .")
Oskar Fischinger. *Light Area, Motion in Space*, 1944. Oil on board, 31 5/8 x 38 7/8 in. (80.33 x 98.74 cm). The San Diego Museum of Art; Museum purchase with funds provided anonymously, 2007.229. Courtesy the Fischinger Trust.

"On Ice"
Abraham Walkowitz. *Isadora Duncan*, 1912. Graphite on paper, 10 1/2 x 7 3/4 in. (26.67 x 19.69 cm). The San Diego Museum of Art; Gift of Mr. and Mrs. Norton S. Walbridge. Also John Sloan, Isadora Duncan, 1915. Etching on laid paper, 8 7/8 x 7 5/16 in. (22.54 x 18.57 cm). The San Diego Museum of Art; Bequest of Earle W. Grant.

"Equivalents" ("With sun rising . . .")
René Magritte. *The Shadows*, 1966. Oil on canvas, 25 11/16 in. x 31 7/8 in. (65.25 cm x 80.96 cm). The San Diego Museum of Art; Gift of Mr. and Mrs. Norton S. Walbridge, 1976.205. Copyright © 2018 C. Herscovici / Artists Rights Society (ARS), New York.

"Developmental Grammar" ("I'm a guitar . . .")
Alexei Jawlensky. *Abstract Head: Inner Vision*, 1923. Oil on board, 16 3/8 x 12 1/2 in. (41.59 x 31.75 cm). The San Diego Museum of Art; Gift of Earle W. Grant in memory of Dalzell Hatfield, 1964.70. Copyright © 2018 Artists Rights Society (ARS), New York.

"And Now I Am Their Song"
Lyre, 19th century. Bone, wood, hair, and vegetable fiber, 47 cm. Musée de la musique; Collection Pauline Tarn.

"Arse Poetica"
Follower of Jean-Baptiste-Siméon Chardin. *Monkey Antiquarian*, after 1740. Oil on canvas, 15 5/8 x 12 7/16 in. (39.69 x 31.59 cm). The San Diego Museum of Art; Gift of Mr. and Mrs. William R. Timken, 1930.55.

"Audio Tour for Wherever You Are" ("Look up . . .")
Frantisek Kupka. *The Beginning of Life*, 1900–1903. Colored aquatint on paper, 34.5 x 34.7 cm. Centre Pompidou; Don Eugénie Kupka, 1963. Copyright © 2018 Artists Rights Society (ARS), New York / ADAGP, Paris.

"The Last Ocean"
Frantisek Kupka. *Blue Space*, circa 1912. Oil on canvas, 26 1/8 x 26 1/8 in. (66.36 x 66.36 cm). The San Diego Museum of Art; Museum purchase through the Earle W. Grant Endowment Fund, 1978.4. Copyright © 2018 Artists Rights Society (ARS), New York / ADAGP, Paris.

"Developmental Grammar" ("I have a secret . . .")
Eugène Delacroix. *Hamlet Tries to Follow His Father's Ghost*, 1835. Lithograph, 10 1/8 x 8 in. (25.7 x 20.3 cm). The Metropolitan Museum of Art; Rogers Fund, 1922.

"Abide with Me"
Christian Rohlfs. *Nude*, 1911. Oil on canvas, 23 3/4 x 20 in. (60.33 x 50.8 cm). The San Diego Museum of Art; Gift of the Estate of Vance E. Kondon and Elisabeth Giesberger, 2011.127.

"Developmental Grammar / Equivalents"
George Inness. *Farm Landscape, Cattle in Pasture, Sunset Nantucket*, circa 1883. Oil on panel, 20 x 30 in. (50.8 x 76.2 cm). The San Diego Museum of Art; Bequest of Mrs. Henry A. Everett, 1938.31.

"Leda and . . ."
Alexander Archipenko. *Leda and the Swan*, circa 1938. Bronze, 13 x 5 5/8 x 4 1/8 in. (33.02 x 14.29 x 10.48 cm). The San Diego Museum of Art; Bequest of Margot W. Marsh, 1995.37. Copyright © 2018 Estate of Alexander Archipenko / Artists Rights Society (ARS), New York.

"Bibliographic Research"
Edward Burne-Jones. *Female Nude*, no date. Graphite on paper, 10 9/16 x 5 13/16 in. (26.83 x 14.76 cm). The San Diego Museum of Art; Gift of the Trustees of the Estate of Mrs. Julius Wangenheim, 1948.55.

"Developmental Grammar" ("That tree burned . . .")
Emil Nolde. *Stormy Sky of Frisian Farmhouse*, circa 1935. Watercolor on paper, 11 5/8 x 13 1/8 in. (29.53 x 33.34 cm). The San Diego Museum of Art; Gift of Mr. and Mrs. Norton S. Walbridge, 1991.17.

"Deaccessioning"
Nainsukh. *Waiting for Her in "Love's Sacred Thicket."* India, Guler, last quarter of the 18th century. Opaque watercolor and gold on paper, 6 25/32 x 10 21/32 in. (17.2 x 27.1 cm). The San Diego Museum of Art; Edwin Binney 3rd Collection, 1990.1270.

"Snot Epistemology (Part I)"
Diego Rivera. *The Hands of Dr. Moore*, 1940. Oil on canvas, 18 x 22 in. (45.72 x 55.88 cm). The San Diego Museum of Art; Bequest of Mrs. E. Clarence Moore, 1970.20. Copyright © 2018 Banco de México Diego Rivera Frida Kahlo Museums Trust, Mexico, D.F. / Artists Rights Society (ARS), New York.

"Snot Epistemology (Part II)"
Joan Miró. *Woman, Bird, Constellations*, 1974. Oil on canvas, 24 x 19 7/8 in. (60.96 x 50.48 cm). The San Diego Museum of Art; Gift of Sol Price in honor of his Wife, Helen, 2008.246. Copyright © Successió Miró / Artists Rights Society (ARS), New York / ADAGP, Paris 2018.

"Audio Tour for Wherever You Are" ("Find the smallest thing . . .")
François Fiedler. *The fire guides all throughout everything . . .*, 1973. Etching, 11 7/8 x 7 1/2 in. (30.16 x 19.05 cm). The San Diego Museum of Art; Gift of Dan and Clo Kramer-Vanesco, 2001.22.19.

"Equivalents" ("The banked facade . . .")
Gutzon Borglum. *Awakening*, 1911. Marble, 34 1/4 x 15 1/4 x 15 in. (87 x 38.74 x 38.1 cm). The San Diego Museum of Art; Gift of Mr. and Mrs. Archer M. Huntington, 1925.2.

"Eat Eat"
Thomas Hart Benton. *After Many Days*, 1940. Tempera and oil on canvas, 31 x 21 in. (78.74 x 53.34 cm). The San Diego Museum of Art; Museum purchase through the Earle W. Grant Acquisition Fund, 1975.3. Copyright © Benton Testamentary Trusts/UMB Bank Trustee/Licensed by VAGA, New York, NY.

"Fire Season" ("How the teeth . . .")
Krishna and the cowherds enter Agasura's mouth, from the Bhagavata Purana ("Ancient Text of the Lord"). India, Datia, circa 1800. Opaque watercolor and gold on paper, 11 13/16 x 14 7/8 in. (30 x 37.8 cm). The San Diego Museum of Art; Edwin Binney 3rd Collection, 1990.994.

"Curing Olives"
Paulo Caliari, known as Veronese. *Apollo and Daphne*, circa 1560–65. Oil on canvas, 43 1/16 x 44 5/8 in. (109.38 x 113.35 cm). The San Diego Museum of Art; Gift of Anne R. and Amy Putnam, 1945.27.

"Fire Season" ("Two fires burn . . .")
After Hendrick Goltzius. *Prometheus Making Man and Animating Him with Fire from Heaven*, 1589. Engraving, 6 7/8 x 10 1/16 in. (17.46 x 25.56 cm). The San Diego Museum of Art; Gift of Norman Leitman and Todd Butler, 2004.133.2.

"Equivalents" ("Rain slicks . . .")
Utagawa Toyokuni II. *Night Rain at Ōyama*, from the series *Eight Famous Views of Kanagawa*, circa 1830. Polychrome woodblock print on paper, 9 1/2 x 14 5/16 in. (24.1 x 36.4 cm). The Metropolitan Museum of Art; Rogers Fund, 1922.

"False Equivalents"
John Martin. *The Fall of the Rebel Angels*, *Paradise Lost*, Book 1, Line 44, undated. Etching, 7 1/2 x 6 in. (19.05 x 15.24 cm). The Blanton Museum of Art; purchased through the generosity of the Still Water Foundation, 1996.

"Push"
Simon Vouet. *Aeneas and His Family Fleeing Troy*, circa 1635–40. Oil on canvas, 55 1/4 x 43 5/16 in. (140.34 x 110.01 cm). The San Diego Museum of Art; Museum purchase, 1987.124.

"Commuted"
Maurice Braun. *Cuyamaca Mountains*, circa 1920. Oil on canvas, 16 x 20 in. (40.64 x 50.8 cm). The San Diego Museum of Art; Bequest of Etta Anna Schwieder.

"Fire Season" ("The stripes are red . . .")
A lion made from calligraphy. India, circa 1800. Opaque watercolor on paper, 5 29/32 x 8 1/16 in. (15 x 20.5 cm). The San Diego Museum of Art; Edwin Binney 3rd Collection, 1990.577.

Acknowledgments

Grateful acknowledgment to the editors of the following journals where these poems first appeared:

> *Hobart*: "That Saying" and "Sod, Stars"
> *Juked*: "Snot Epistemology (Part 1 and Part 2)"
> *Zócalo Public Square*: "On Ice"

And to *ZYZZYVA*, who in publishing the precursor to the series gave me confidence to keep working in this direction.

My gratitude to Jeffrey Levine, Jim Schley, Marie Gauthier, and the Tupelo Press staff, as well as Carol Frost, for this unexpected gift. Thank you, thank you.

Heartfelt thanks to all the colleagues and friends who've shared work-life over the years, especially my fellow independent bookslingers, museum cohort, and the writers I've learned so much from at Indiana University and University of California–Irvine. Special thanks to Michelle Latiolais, James McMichael, Tony Ardizzone, Bob Bledsoe, Cathy Bowman, Ross Gay, Debra Kang Dean, Maurice Manning, Romayne Rubinas Dorsey, Samrat Upadhyay, Devin Becker, and Sonya Rhie Mace, and to the memory of Don Belton. My thanks to the San Diego Museum of Art and the other institutions that shared images of works of art from their collections. To Vernon Ng, for being a longtime guiding light, and a better friend than anyone has rights to expect. To my family, for putting up with me, and occasionally letting me write about you and your dental incidents, and to Mark and Chris for the Granny Flat Writer's Residency.

And to Lauren, in all things, forever, for all things—including these two: Nora and Alice. It is such a joy to watch you write your stories.

Other Books from Tupelo Press

Silver Road: Essays, Maps & Calligraphies (hybrid memoir), Kazim Ali

A Certain Roughness in Their Syntax (poems), Jorge Aulicino, translated by Judith Filc

Flight (poems), Chaun Ballard

Another English: Anglophone Poems from Around the World (anthology),
    edited by Catherine Barnett and Tiphanie Yanique

Personal Science (poems), Lillian-Yvonne Bertram

Everything Broken Up Dances (poems), James Byrne

Almost Human (poems), Thomas Centolella

Land of Fire (poems), Mario Chard

New Cathay: Contemporary Chinese Poetry (anthology), edited by Ming Di

Calazazza's Delicious Dereliction (poems), Suzanne Dracius, translated by Nancy Naomi Carlson

Hallowed (poems), Patricia Fargnoli

Gossip and Metaphysics: Russian Modernist Poetry and Prose (anthology),
    edited by Katie Farris, Ilya Kaminsky, and Valzhyna Mort

Xeixa: Fourteen Catalan Poets (anthology), edited by Marlon L. Fick and Francisca Esteve

Leprosarium (poems), Lise Goett

My Immaculate Assassin (novel), David Huddle

Dancing in Odessa (poems), Ilya Kaminsky

A God in the House: Poets Talk About Faith (interviews),
    edited by Ilya Kaminsky and Katherine Towler

At the Gate of All Wonder (novel), Kevin McIlvoy

The Cowherd's Son (poems), Rajiv Mohabir

Marvels of the Invisible (poems), Jenny Molberg

Canto General: Song of the Americas (poems), Pablo Neruda,
    translated by Mariela Griffor and Jeffrey Levine

Ex-Voto (poems), Adélia Prado, translated by Ellen Doré Watson

The Life Beside This One (poems), Lawrence Raab

Intimate: An American Family Photo Album (hybrid memoir), Paisley Rekdal

Thrill-Bent (novel), Jan Richman

Innocent Eye: A Passionate Look at Contemporary Art (essays), Patricia Rosoff

Dirt Eaters (poems), Eliza Rotterman

Good Bones (poems), Maggie Smith

The Perfect Life (essays), Peter Stitt

Swallowing the Sea (essays), Lee Upton

feast gently (poems), G. C. Waldrep

Republic of Mercy (poems), Sharon Wang

Legends of the Slow Explosion (essays), Baron Wormser

See our complete list at www.tupelopress.org